YEAR

J.R. MAHON

Design by Supan Creative Co.

Printed in the United States of America.

THE PEOPLE IN YEAR

DIANE MAHON - Without you this would have never happened. THANK YOU! I LOVE YOU!

MIA ROSE - The laughter and annoyance is always perfect.

GELATO - Your curiosity keeps me in the game.

Z - Your willingness to be all in, all the time, makes you great!

ROB SUPAN - Best friend and spiritual backstop. Your design gave this collection life.

TRICIA SUPAN - Your friendship with Diane creates happy tears.

SHERYL FLEISHER - My spiritual director. Thank you for saving my life.

BRANDON & ABBEY IRWIN - You are family!

GREG VANDEGRIFT - Thank you for the many lessons on grammar and word choice. I'm sure you'll find a few more mistakes. In fact, I'm counting on it!

BRETT AKAGI - Grateful for your incredible friendship.

MICHELLE FLUKE - Your encouragement helped me hear my voice.

JON MIKLAS - The exact opposite of me and man, do I love you!

PAMELA BESCH - Sister!

TRINITY JORDAN - Thank you for never saying, "No."

KERSTIN LINDQUIST - The world doesn't have enough clothes!!! Your support got me here!

DAN ALLEMEIER - I know who you married. Prayers to you every day! Thank you for the friendship and support.

CHAD LAUTERBACH - Your example helped me back into the rooms.

MARK DAVIDSON - My little brother, thank you for the friendship.

KAREN AND PAUL FORGET - For all the holiday dinners and California laughs.

JAKE-A-HEIDI BLAKNEY - Our insanity has never phased you. You both must be nuts. Love you!

DALLAS BILLINGTON - I love the way you dress and smell. Your faith is incredible to watch.

TONY MITCHELL - Old-timer, disciple-maker, friend. Thank you!

CHRIS DANLEY - So much of this started with you. I'm smiling knowing you are in my life. Kiss Michael for me.

DON & JOAN MAHON, DONNA & JACK ANDERSON - Thank you for the mothering and fathering.

CLIENTS AND DIRECTEES - Thank you for y our trust and willingness to go deep.

INSTAGRAM, FACEBOOK AND TWITTER FRIENDS - Thank you for all the likes, DM's, comments and follows; and thank you to those who write and share your life with me.

PREFACE

IN JANUARY 2017 the intention was to write a second book. The expectation? It would take three months and would be a regular book, like all other books. I would write about the insanity of my faith, adopting strangers, marriage and the giant mistakes I've made learning to love. What happened is what happens when you include your soul in the creative process; the exact opposite. What's in front of you was not my design or aim. In front of you is an act of contemplation that spun completely out of control and birthed 365 individual sentences over 365 days. The Greek call work like this *logia*, after the word *logion*, which is a term for sayings or aphorisms. I call this work YEAR.

The creative process is a wonderful, mysterious expression of mind, body and soul. Those who fight its power often lose the very essence of what needs to be created. "Who the hell writes individual sentences as a book?" I would tell myself, while staring at a page filled with weird extractions from my morning silence and contemplations. I grew concerned. Forming paragraphs became a struggle, but forming thoughts filled with 5-15 words was like riding a bike. It felt easy, natural and innate; and the only thing coming out. Yet as a work or project it was a massive cosmic joke at the time, that translated, "I was a joke."

After a few months of bending away from what seemed natural, I gave up and joined the sentences. I started listening intentionally to their tone, meaning and guidance. I gained new awareness. I lost the need to prove, convince, and argue. I was learning as I wrote; transforming as I gave energy to new thoughts and I became obsessed. I was quantifying what I was thinking, feeling and contemplating about God, the universe and that dusty 30-year-old named Jesus. For 12 months every morning I studied, listened, prayed, meditated, contemplated and emptied out. My iPhone became my notebook and social media my outlet. I developed a small following over the interwebs of curious friends, strangers and those dedicated to transformation: Christians, Hindus, Jews, Atheists, Buddhists, Sufis and a whole lot of cryptocurrency and personal fitness folks. All this to say, you never know who is watching. I gave myself two metrics along the way: Always look past the temptation to anchor in certainty, and have nothing to prove and nothing to lose. Frankly at times, the process was a pain in the ass, as it introduced several, if not many opportunities to look deep inside myself, exposing both the sorrow and joy of being John Mahon.

Where was it coming from and why did it pick this season? I blame it on my spiritual chase to know God, to know me, to know you, to know earth and learn to love them all. I also blame the dozens of people I care for as a Spiritual Director, who every day help me see myself in ways I thought not possible. Call me naive, but six months into writing YEAR, and a few decades of following God, it never fully occurred to me that Spirit was aggressively bleeding into what was being written. It was only when I saw YEAR in a word document that I stopped and marveled at some of the places it takes you. It was like a hostile spiritual creative takeover. At times, I was simply unaware of the beauty unfolding in front of me. I stopped caring where it came from and gave thanks that it was here.

YEAR is not new emerging thought. It is not tied down, and does not read as rules or processes needing to be followed. I was lead into YEAR by the quiet and peaceful voice that has been with me since I was a kid. I anchored much of my study among the teachings of Jesus. His blazing passion to interrupt the human ego has attracted me for decades. As you engage this book I encourage you to set the words, phrases and sentences alongside your own spiritual practice. Whether you meditate, contemplate, pray, practice yoga or forms of silence; take this collection with you and allow the words to run among your faith and daily life. Lose the dogmas of your religion, the ego of your belief, and be attentive to the voice that dwells in you. Shrink back from any one position that keeps you from your fellow man and difference of faith. Be ready for new awareness and consciousness. Allow spiritual self discovery to fund the desire to transform. Know it's O.K. to seek something you can't put a name on or even find words for. Form opinions, thoughts, new beliefs and encourage curiosity and community. Finally, give yourself a giant spiritual break and know faith is not simply behavioral modification or the power to convert millions. Faith is the very foundation of love and love holds the beauty of who you are.

WELCOME TO YEAR.

J.R. Mahon
Spiritual Director
@jrmahon

REST IS THE REBELLION.

002

YEAR

Happiness is not contingent on... *him,*
her,
they,
them,
or it.

003

YEAR

GOD NEEDS DISCIPLES,
NOT ETERNITY POLICE.

004

YEAR

COMMIT YOURSELF
TO THE NEEDS
OF OTHERS.

005

■ YEAR

Your church,
synagogue,
political affiliation,
power,
fame,
or social status

have nothing to do with how you change the world.

“Therefore go and make disciples;”

not picket,

or bitch,

or moan and complain.

007

YEAR

God has no expe

ctation of belief.

008

YEAR

LOVE UNDEFENDED.

NOTHING TO LOSE, NOTHING TO PROVE.

010

■ YEAR

How that
homeless person
spends that dollar

AIN'T YOUR BUSINESS.

Salvation isn't
community sameness.

It's pure, unadulterated
personal liberation.

.012
YEAR

FEAR *is not yours to* **KEEP.**

.013
YEAR

MYSTERY SCRAPS DUALITY AND GIVES BIRTH TO PEACE.

.014 YEAR

Spiritual maturity
is not built on
rules, regulation
or process.
It's built on the
backs of sorrow
and joy.

.015 YEAR

Your small relationships define **HOW YOU LOVE**.

YEAR 016

SAY SOME THING

017 YEAR

KILL

BUSY

018
YEAR

IF NOT DOING PRAYER PLANS OR DAILY VERSE STUDIES IS PRODUCING GUILT OR SHAME,

STOP TRYING TO DO THEM.

019
YEAR

GOD'S GOOD WITH YOU JUST THINKING ABOUT HIM.

In fact, He'd prefer that.

020 ■ YEAR

You don't need God's permission.

021

YEAR

NEGOTIATING DURING PRAYER IS SPIRITUAL MASTURBATION.

022
YEAR

EXPECTATIONS
without words become
RESENTMENTS.

023

YEAR

You *LEARN*
to love.

024

YEAR

Loving others requires the consciousness of UNSELFISHNESS, FORGIVENESS, and TEACHABILITY.

025

YEAR

MOVE FORWARD

026 YEAR

VULNERABILITY

is the currency of the soul.

027

YEAR

YOU'RE NEVER TOO OLD.

028 ■ YEAR

Tell on
yourself.

029

YEAR

BE LOVE ON THE MOVE: { creative,
flexible
& full of
faithful
evolution.

Going to church;
Being the church: **TWO DIFFERENT THINGS.**

031

YEAR

PERSEVERANCE
BIRTHS MATURITY

032

■ YEAR

TAKE ON PROBLEMS

PEOPLE FI

034

YEAR

Seek God

ST.

Not safety, security
or understanding.

YEAR

Success is anchored in *hope* and *rests* on what you can't see.

036

YEAR

Faith allows *failure* and is the greatest measure of *success*.

037 YEAR

Vulnerability **KILLS** social media envy

SELF-CENTEREDNESS DISSOLVES DIVINE LOVE.

ADOPT
NEED

040

YEAR

The ***incentive***
for ***accountability***
is ***friendship***.

041 ■ YEAR

PRAYERS AREN'T **TRANSACTIONS.**

042 YEAR

Jesus never sat in the past, nor

allowed the future to drive fear.

043 ■ YEAR

The most valuable gift you can give:

TIME.

044 ■ YEAR

You are not struggling, you are

LIVING.

THE GOOD SAMARITAN DIDN'T KNOW THE MAN HE SAVED.

HE DIDN'T QUESTION HIS TROUBLE, JUDGE HIS CONDITION OR CONTEMPLATE THE COST OF SACRIFICE.

046

YEAR

Doubt, wonder, and questioning are central and essential to faith.

047

YEAR

Earth as **"being,"** not rental property.

048 YEAR

Sorrow builds New Life.

049 ■ YEAR

Great fear will produce

GREAT PRAYER

YOU ARE NOT LOOKING FOR A

MOMENTARY STATE OF CONSCIOUSNESS.

YOU'RE SEEKING A WAY OF LIFE.

051 ■ YEAR

The desire to be **loved**, **known**, and **touched** is real.

052 ■ YEAR

EMBRACING YOUR HUMANITY PRODUCES **LIFE,**

NOT METHODOLOGIES FOR TAMING BEHAVIOR.

Divine presence is uncontrollable.
Feeling out of control is part of the deal.

THE TRINITY is not measuring your life in terms of **SUCCESS OR FAILURE.**

055 ■ YEAR

REST

The metric for rest is rest;

not the amount of it.

SELF-GUIDED SPIRITUALITY

IS

SOUL IMPRISONMENT

.057 ■ YEAR

COMMUNITY
and **GUIDANCE**
are essential to
SPIRITUAL
TRANSFORMATION.

058

■ YEAR

Allow **SILENCE** to say everything.

059

YEAR

FEAR KNOWS WHAT'S NEXT.

060

■ YEAR

PAIN
IS AN INVITATION TO
LOVE.

190 ■ YEAR

The greatest
love producing moments of your life
will come through pain.

062 ■ YEAR

Forgiveness is social activism.

063

YEAR

Waiting for God means actively pursuing Him,

not bitching about circumstances.

064

YEAR

The question isn't whether you're going to

HEAVEN OR HELL.

The question is are you going to create

HEAVEN OR HELL?

065 ■ YEAR

Every now and then ask, **"What do you think of me?"**

066

■ YEAR

Salvation is not behavioral modification.

067 YEAR

Your body isn't
simply delightful or
disdained reflection.

068

YEAR

069

YEAR

Be eager to be last.

070 YEAR

Believe above what you know.

PRACTICE STUDY.

Allow curiosity to drive it
and be open to its finding.

.072 ■ YEAR

Jesus is content.

073 ■ YEAR

The prodigal son, beyond realizing he'd been a jackass, accepted his father's love. That alone will be the hardest thing we do with our lives.

.074
YEAR

"Spiritual power grabs"
exclude you from
the mind of Christ.

.075
YEAR

Seeking **POWER**
over **PEOPLE**
will never yield peace.

.076 ■ YEAR

EVERYTHING will have a
death, burial and *resurrection.*

077
YEAR

PRAYER

– Reflecting His grace.

MEDITATION

– Allowing His grace within.

CONTEMPLATION

– Standing in wonder of His grace.

078 ■ YEAR

Your walk
with God
needs to
look human.

079 YEAR

JESUS DIDN'T **ARGUE.**

PEACE
RUNS ALONGSIDE
FAITH.

081

YEAR

Spiritual exhaustion
comes from thinking you can
work yourself into relationship with God.

082 YEAR

CONTROL **KILLS FAITH**

CONVINCE NO ONE.

084 YEAR

YOU WERE CREATED TO BE LOVED

085

YEAR

Don't be right. **BE PRESENT.**

086 YEAR

JOY + SORROW

are the markers of being fully alive.

087 YEAR

SURRENDER IS

not the act of being beat, but the act of being

FULLY ALIVE.

YEAR

EMPTY YOURSELF

089

YEAR

ANTICIPATE THE
NEEDS** OF **OTHERS.

090
■ YEAR

MOVE PAST

the judgment of

PEOPLE'S ETERNITY

091

YEAR

REDEMPTION
OFFERS
THE
WORLD

**THE
VALUE
OF OWNING
MISTAKES.**

092

YEAR

Your behavior will change
when you lose the idea that
God's only job is to correct it.

.093 ■ YEAR

The absence of process & rule give way to spiritual transformation.

.094 ■ YEAR

The blessing of sorrow is having experienced great joy.

095
YEAR

HATE WHAT BREAKS YOU **+ LOVE ITS OUTCOME.**

096

YEAR

The indulgences of Jesus had little to do with *security, power & pleasure.*

097 YEAR

JESUS KNOWS WHAT YOU KNOW.

Give not from your **WEALTH**, but from what you **PROTECT**.

099

■ YEAR

LETTING GO INVOLVES THE HUMILITY

TO KNOW YOU HAVE NO CONTROL.

FEAR

produces

WISDOM

when you walk through it.

YOUR FAITH
should never determine
YOUR FRIENDSHIPS.

CHRISTIANITY CEASES TO ACT ON ITS CALL TO LOVE WHEN BELIEFS PIT HUMAN AGAINST HUMAN.

God waits for you…

patiently,

longingly,

happily,

lovingly,

and will never stop.

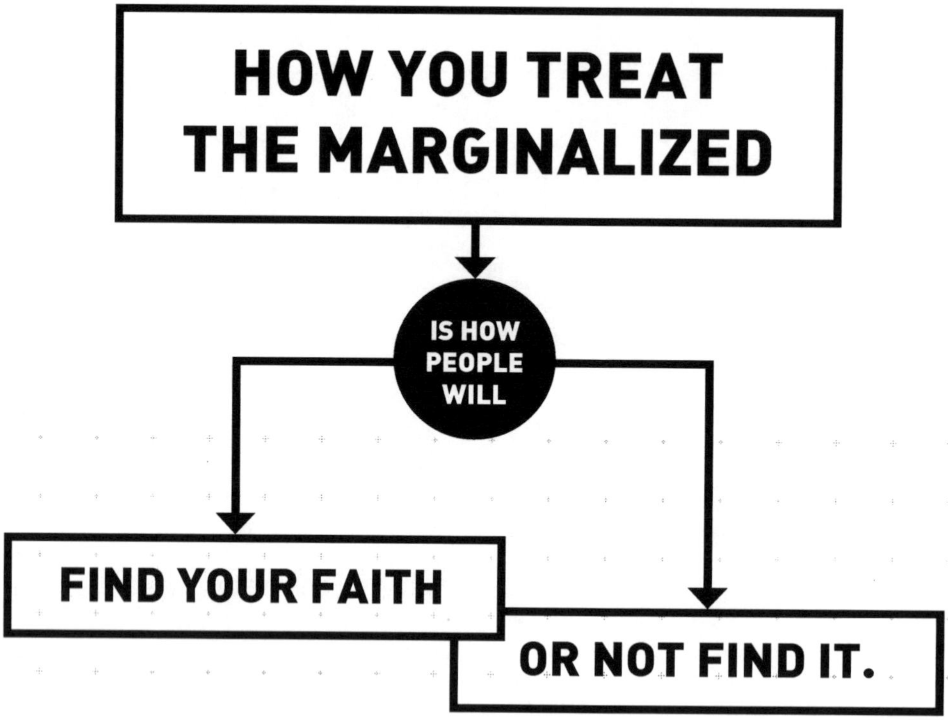

HOW YOU TREAT THE MARGINALIZED

IS HOW PEOPLE WILL

FIND YOUR FAITH

OR NOT FIND IT.

Jesus has little regard for social vanity.

BE POWERFULLY, WONDERFULLY, ORDINARY.

106

YEAR

Leadership doesn't produce disciples.

Powerful undefended humility produces disciples.

BE LEADERSHIP FREE.

107

YEAR

Healing pain can mean leaving the one thing you perceive as life giving.

THE MYSTERY OF GOD SHOULD PUSH EVERY THEOLOGICAL BOUNDARY YOU'VE EVER ENCOUNTERED

109

YEAR

[Jesus didn't guilt or shame.]

YEAR

THE GATEWAY TO CHRIST ISN'T ADMITTING SIN; IT'S THE AWARENESS OF GREATER LOVE.

God isn't gunning for you.

Whatever is going on today,
He is with you,
He is in you,
He is loving you.

YEAR 112

CREATING PEACE MIGHT MEAN YOU DON'T

113 ■ YEAR

{ *Take a deep breath.* }

You don't have to ***perform, get it right***
or even ***come close*** to looking like Jesus.

YEAR

RECONCILIATION IS THE **ABSENCE OF EXPECTATION.**

RESURRECTION ALLOWS **SORROW AND JOY** TO BECOME **HOPE**.

116

YEAR

FEAR, WORRY, REMORSE.

THEY NEED YOUR COOPERATION; NOT NEGLECT.

117 YEAR

You can't believe alone.

118 ■ YEAR

The 12 disciples weren't trained for leadership. They were called to transform and love.

+

YOUR HUNGER

FOR GOD SHOULD BE

SATISFIED BY

YOUR DESIRE

TO QUESTION HIM.

+

120

YEAR

God saw all that
he had made and
it was very good.

Adopt the theology of good.

121

YEAR

SACRIFICE IS TEAM PLAY.

122

YEAR

It's not, "We are bad and God makes us good."

It's, "We are loved and always have been."

123

YEAR

SPIRITUAL TRANSFORMATION IS THE DEATH OF EGO.

124

YEAR

SECURITY, POWER AND FAME

will not touch the soul.

125 ■ YEAR

Every day God scans the horizon looking for you.

126 ■ YEAR

Discernment is the quiet discovery of

ANOTHER'S SOUL.

■ YEAR

TOUCH THE UNLOVED.

You know who they are because a lot of your day is spent ignoring them.

VULNERABILITY

is the gateway to a mature and lasting faith.

129
YEAR

PEACE

is predicated on how you value humanity.

The adoption of love is
messy,
unchained,
chaotic,
uncontrolled,
painful,
sorrowful;
yet opens us to the most freeing
human experience we can have:
losing ourselves for others.

131

YEAR

Love isn't what you get; it's what you're willing to give.

YOUR YEARNING
TO BE FULLY ALIVE
WITH GOD
WILL BE SATISFIED.

SPIRITUAL TRANSFORMATION IS PURSUIT.

134 YEAR

FAME CONSUMES
THE DESIRE
TO BE LOVED.

God
LIVES AND LOVES
among your
polar opposites.

136

■ YEAR

Peter denied Jesus three times.
The third time the Lord turned
and looked at Peter,
not disappointed or pissed,
but in complete mercy-filled
understanding for the
condition of his
terrified heart.

137 YEAR

THE PEOPLE YOU SEE TODAY:

Recognize them, allow them to be known by you, give them your undivided attention, help them walk away feeling wanted.

YOUR SEARCH FOR GOD
IS FUELED BY
HIS SEARCH FOR YOU.

139
YEAR

The people you meet today:
Allow yourself to be known,
give them your story,
help them walk away
with a piece of you.

Our beliefs don't make us divine;
the awareness of God's creation does.

141 YEAR

**AVOID WHAT YOU LOVE.
RECEIVE WHAT YOU HATE.**

FORGIVE AT INFINITE.

143
YEAR

Move beyond platitudes.

Comfortability is not the call of Christ.

145 ■ YEAR

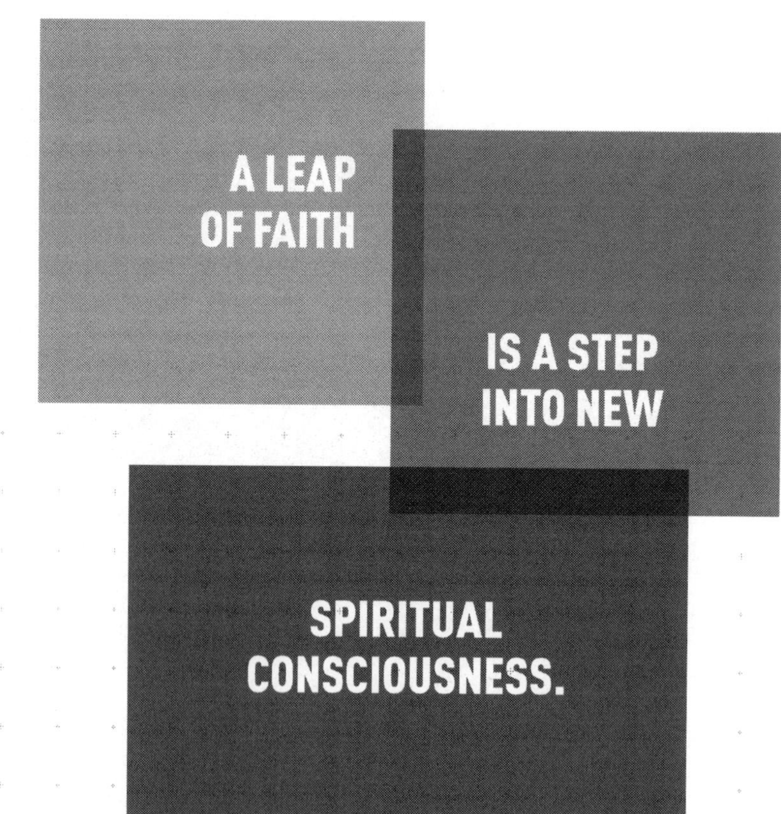

146

■ YEAR

Spiritual awakening begins
when you delight in your humanity.

147

YEAR

Sex is a mere dot on the map of marriage.

Forgiveness, on the other hand,
is the paper on which the map is drawn.

Prayer is the **PRACTICE OF PRESENCE,**

not the **EXHAUST OF SELFISH DESIRE.**

149 ■ YEAR

Eliminating parts of your story
or ***ignoring*** parts of your story
denies the gift of new life.

150 ■ YEAR

THE MYSTERY OF GOD
KILLS EGO.

“I don’t know,”

should be illuminating, not humiliating.

YEAR

**Having the mind of Christ
is a selfless consciousness to all.**

153 ■ YEAR

Your insistence to be right stunts faith.

154 ■ YEAR

ALLOW DISCOVERY THAT MOVES YOU TO HUMILITY.

Allow opposition a third way.

YEAR

The lie isn't, **"GOD'S NOT REAL."**

It's, **"YOU CAN BE GOD."**

PETER DENIED JESUS THREE TIMES

{ ...yet planted a church on every corner of the world. }

DOUBT IS THE FABRIC OF **FAITH.**

If avoiding hell is your centerpiece of theology, **CHANGE YOUR CENTER.**

RULES & BEHAVIOR

ARE NOT THE CENTERING POINT FOR

SPIRITUAL TRANSFORMATION.

.161

YEAR

TAKE A BREAK FROM
YOUR OPINION AND STORY.

.162

YEAR

REBUILD CHURCH. STOP LEAVING.

■ YEAR

YOUR COMMODITY should be silence,
NOT INFORMATION.

164 YEAR

JESUS WAS ARRESTED.

165

■ YEAR

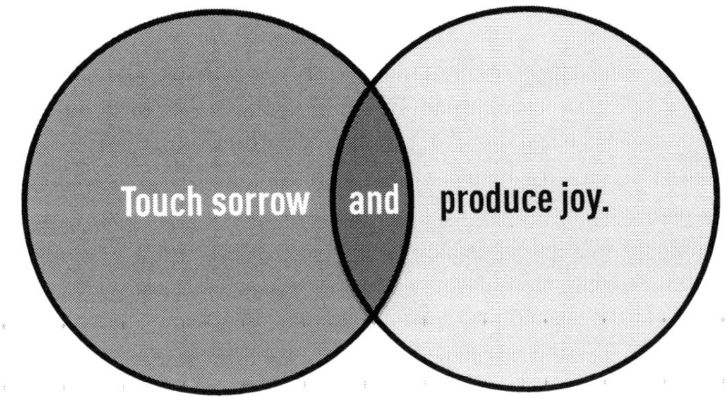

166

YEAR

THE WORK THAT SURROUNDS YOUR FAITH
COULD BE SCREWING YOU.

Be all in.

[Luxury is weight.]

169

YEAR

OFFEND like Jesus.

170
YEAR

YOUR WEAKNESS IS YOUR TEACHER.

171
YEAR

YOUR MIRROR IS YOUR HISTORY.

172
YEAR

Jesus loved the soul, ***not the gathering.***

173

YEAR

Jesus wrestled with fear.

174 ■ YEAR

THERE IS NO FEAR IN LOVE.

175 ■ YEAR

FEAR DOES NOT DECIDE TO CONTROL YOU.

THAT'S ON YOU.

176 YEAR

SHAMING PEOPLE'S FEAR

KEEPS THEM AFRAID.

177

YEAR

Fear runs in the family.
Allow love to cover it.

Service is not vacation,
temporary or seasonal.

179

YEAR

Embracing your darkness is

spiritual maturity.

God loves dirty hands.

181 YEAR

Patience is a space of reunion

WITH GOD.

182 YEAR

The powerless remain forever in the

HEART OF GOD.

Recognizing powerlessness gives birth to the soul.

DESTINATION is not a place; it's EMBRACE.

185

■ YEAR

GET OFF THE INTERNET.

186 YEAR

Jesus doesn't need you to be **JESUS** at work.

He needs you to be **YOU** at work.

.187 YEAR

YOUR VALUE + WORTH
have nothing to do with
YOU THINKING THERE IS
something wrong with you.

188 ■ YEAR

Allow silence to be

TODAY'S EVENT.

---

189 ■ YEAR

God's not *expecting* **ANYTHING** today.

If your pursuit of faith
looks + feels
like the daily grind,

STOP!

YEAR

Poverty of spirit is **freedom from ego.**

192 YEAR

Allow weakness to liberate you.

Christ didn't come to increase your

He came

chances of getting into heaven.

to help you lose yourself to love.

Give yourself to the needs of others.

195 ■ YEAR

EVERYTHING WILL NEVER BE ENOUGH.

196

YEAR

BIND

YOURSELF

TO LESS.

197

YEAR

If you're arguing about Jesus,

for Jesus, or because of Jesus,

you ain't Jesusing correctly.

.198

YEAR

It’s not a matter of not fearing
people or circumstances.
It’s accepting you will.

199

■ YEAR

VULNERABILITY IS SALUTARY.

SHAME LIVES AND DIES

IN YOUR WILLINGNESS TO UNDERCUT SELFISH DESIRE.

JESUS WENT UNNOTICED FOR

30 YEARS.

HE LIVED A FULL LIFE BEFORE HE TURNED HIS ATTENTION

TO YOU.

202
YEAR

SEXUAL DESIRE HAS NEVER BEEN AT ISSUE.

SELFISH DESIRE WITHOUT LOVE IS THE ISSUE.

203
YEAR

SELFISH SEXUAL DESIRE ***KILLS*** EMOTIONAL INTIMACY.

LOVE IS THE BEDROCK OF SEXUAL DESIRE

Everyone wants to be known.

loved.

THE NEED FOR

SUCCESS, POWER, CONTROL & SELF RELIANCE

WILL NEVER LOOK LIKE JESUS.

The call to God is natural.
It is in you and in those around you.

208 YEAR

DUALITY *serves ego, not faith.*

209 YEAR

RESTORE EACH OTHER.

210 YEAR

TOUCH THE EARTH.

211 ■ YEAR

THE MARKERS OF SPIRITUAL JOURNEY:

faith, humility, love, peace,

sacrifice, forgiveness.

The widow,
the orphan,
the sick,
the poor;

or

the vacation,
the new car,
the membership
or the remodel.

GOD'S NOT AFRAID OF ANYTHING YOU THINK OR FEEL.

214 YEAR

Our allegiance to certainty kills the very faith we claim.

215 ■ YEAR

MYSTERY IS NOT EVIL,
IT'S LIFE GIVING.

216 YEAR

ALLOW BELIEF TO CHANGE.

217 YEAR

PEOPLE NEED YOUR TIME.

218 ■ YEAR

KEEP YOUR MONEY.

[Give folks the blessing of being known.]

219 ■ YEAR

Women can teach,
gays can serve,
and you can have an opinion.

HOW

CONTROLLING HOW YOU LOVE AND WHO YOU LOVE AIN'T LOVE.

LOVE PEOPLE;
DON'T TAME PEOPLE.

YOUR WILLINGNESS TO
PROTECT TITLE, POSITION
AND POWER WILL
NEVER CREATE PEACE.

RISK
LOVE.

224

YEAR

Your faith announces new life.

ALLOW PEOPLE TRANSFORMATION.

226 ■ YEAR

faith passion

FAITH RECOGNIZES THE POSSIBILITIES OF PASSION.

Everything
belongs
to you.

228 ■ YEAR

Jesus didn't love with, **"but..."**

229 YEAR

LOVE WORTH PURSUING... IS LOVE WITHOUT CONTROL.

230

YEAR

DON'T BE DETERMINED BY ECONOMICS

I wish you heartache.

232
YEAR

GRIEVE THE LOSSES OF YOUR PAST.

233
YEAR

WE ARE NOT A PROBLEM FOR GOD.

PREFERENCE, JUDGEMENT & EXCLUSION ARE DEBILITATING.

There is nothing wrong with you.

T'S NONE
OF YOUR
BUSINESS.

237 YEAR

FREE YOURSELF FROM THE MINDS OF OTHERS.

238 ■ YEAR

PRAY YOUR HEART BE REALIZED.

239

■ YEAR

MOTIVATION IS A SPRINT.

PRAYER IS THE JOURNEY.

THERE IS NO DISTANCE BETWEEN

GOD

ALL S

ILLS
PACES.

242 YEAR

You touch God within a single breath.

IF YOU'RE FIGHTING FOR

INFLUENCE, POWER, SECURITY AND TITLE,

YOU'RE FIGHTING THE WRONG THE FIGHT.

244 YEAR

INVISIBLE

ARE SOME OF THE MOST VALUED GIFTS.

Disciple, DON'T HERD.

246

YEAR

Know the hearts you lead.

247

YEAR

BLESSING is the recognition of LOVE.

248

YEAR

SAYING, "**I do,**" IS BEGINNING.

SAYING, "**I forgive you,**" IS LIFE.

249 YEAR

JOY & SORROW come in the same syringe.

BELIEF
SHOULDN'T PUT CONDITIONS ON
LOVE

.251 YEAR

[

There will be times of complete darkness.

Some of which won't make any damn sense.

]

NO SECRETS

253

YEAR

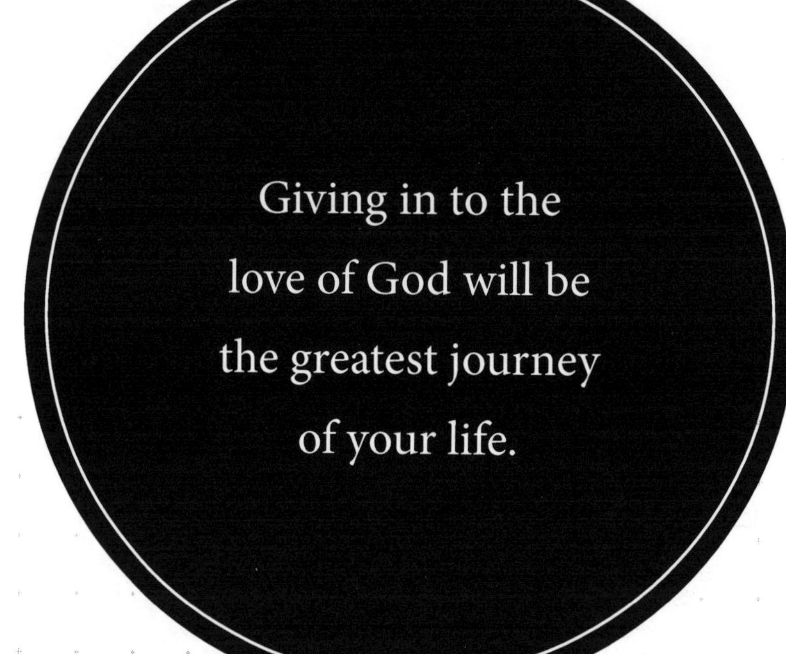
Giving in to the
love of God will be
the greatest journey
of your life.

254

YEAR

ALLOW PAIN TO MATURE INTO LOVE.

255 ■ YEAR

YES,

IT'S POSSIBLE TO LOVE YOURSELF WHEN REJECTED.

256 YEAR

Be interrupted.

257 YEAR

YOUR EGO WILL **NEVER SATISFY** YOUR DESIRE TO BE LOVED.

258 YEAR

MERCY SHATTERS SHAME.

WHATEVER YOU'VE DONE, WHATEVER YOU'VE SAID...

IT'S O.K.

260 YEAR

KEEP YOUR MONEY.

GIVE YOUR BELONGING.

261 ■ YEAR

Christ wasn't out to prove human negligence.

PREOCCUPATION WITH SELF
IS SPIRITUAL VIOLENCE.

Spiritual credit
based on works
ain't a thing.

264 ■ YEAR

FORGIVENESS HAS A PRICE.

You might lose a brother, gain a friend or offend an entire community. The price never trumps the liberation of pain and injection of new life.

265 ■ YEAR

Faith is **HUMILITY**, not **VANITY**.

266 ■ YEAR

There are no **SPIRITUAL MERIT BADGES**.

267 YEAR

We never lose faith.

We struggle with
uncertainty.

268

YEAR

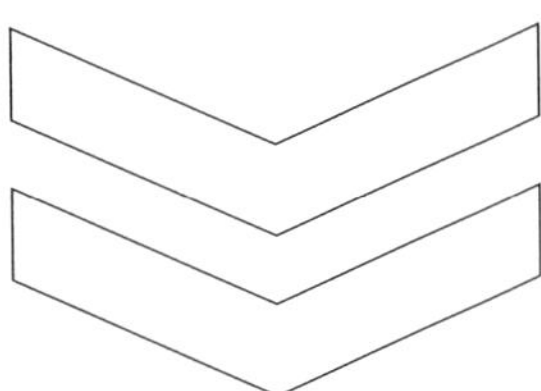

FORGIVENESS SEEKS INTIMACY WITH THE DIVINE.

269 YEAR

CARRY EACH OTHER'S BURDENS.

270 YEAR

TRUST THE SLOW WORK OF GOD.

Keep relationships
alive in **LOVE;**
not alive in **PAIN.**

272 YEAR

Darkness needs friends.

The miracles of Jesus were both liberating and lawless.

274 YEAR

YOUR ATTENTION CREATES LIFE.

275 ■ YEAR

LET ANONYMITY DOMINATE

YOUR DEEDS.

276 YEAR

Your story should start with, **"We…"**

Tend the human heart.

278 YEAR

Willingness to oppose other spiritual practices is bad methodology.

DON'T BE A one-trick spiritual pony

280

YEAR

Allow
RIGOROUS
SELF
examination.

Giving should be planned spontaneity.

Tell the stories that make you cry.

ALLOW
THE
WORLD
YOUR
EXPERIENCE,
STRENGTH
& HOPE.

284 ■ YEAR

Discover the need of a stranger.

WANT YOUR OWN LIFE.

Be teachable.

287 YEAR

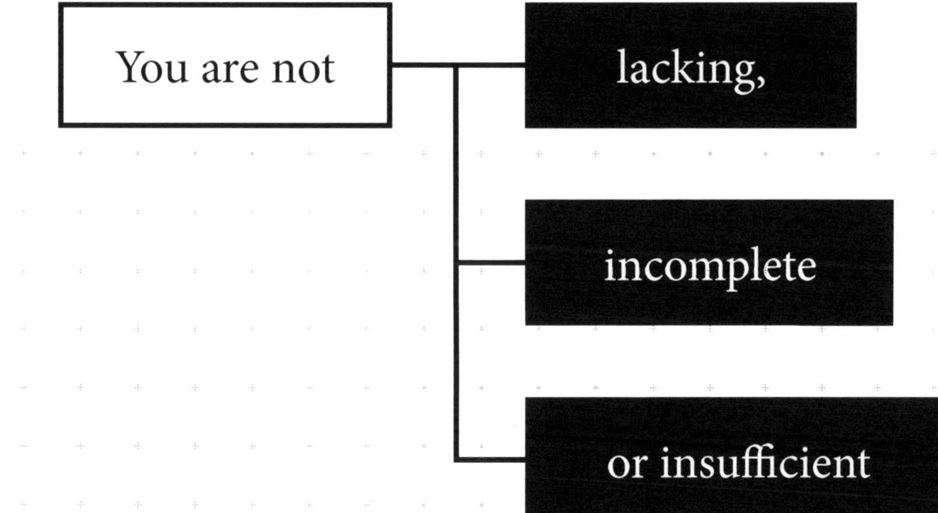

It's not original sin;

it's original love.

289 YEAR

God doesn't see you as wreckage.

290
YEAR

NO MORE GUILTING.
NO MORE SHAMING.

291

YEAR

condition
you to be a

DOORMAT

Faith & celebrity = inch deep, mile wide.

1

2

294 YEAR

Wisdom is sweet to your soul.

.295 YEAR

Define yourself
not by WHO you love,
but IF you love.

296

YEAR

Your voice is louder fear isn't driving

and stronger when
what others hear.

297 ■ YEAR

PLEASING vs SERVING:

one hopes for **RECOGNITION**,
the other creates **COMMUNITY**.

298 YEAR

Anger is a thing after being hurt,
but being **pissed**
should be a **season**
not a lifetime.

299 YEAR

ANGER
LEFT UNCHECKED
BECOMES
SELF RIGHTEOUS
INTOXICATION.

300

■ YEAR

TURN THE COVERAGE OFF

That voice inside of you,
left unchecked will leave you
with regret...

Which is not impossible
to live with but
SUPER uncomfortable.

Jesus targets the ego,
hoping you shave off a bit of that,
"I CAN CONTROL EVERYTHING,"
bullshit.

ASKING FOR HELP
ISN'T ADMITTING DEFEAT...
IT'S WISDOM 101.

TAKE A BREAK. THE MONEY, FAME, AND FORTUNE WILL ALL BE WAITING FOR YOU WHEN YOU GET BACK.

305
YEAR

FORGIVENESS IS ALL ABOUT **YOU.**

306
YEAR

WE **BUILD** OR **BREAK.**

307 YEAR

There was a man who never made mistakes.

He was the worst human ever.

308
YEAR

Perfection

is bullshit.

Originality is lost on those seeking

ATTENTION.

Our collective beauty is not in

THE QUEST FOR PERFECTION,

but the strength found in brokenness.

311 YEAR

WISDOM IS THE DEEP KNOWING OF SELF.

It will haunt you, inspire you and change you.

WHAT WE DON'T DO AND WHO WE DON'T DO IT WITH NEEDS ACCOUNTABILITY.

PAIN IS NOT CREATED EQUAL

SOME PAIN IS THE ALLOWANCE OF NEXT STEPS, SOME PAIN STOPS A GIVEN SEASON AND SOME PAIN DRAWS YOU TO LOVE.

314 ■ YEAR

PAIN AS NECESSITY

NOT AVOIDANCE.

Ego building; **not a thing.**

316 ■ YEAR

You belong to a vast
cosmic love conspiracy
that has nothing
to do with behavior
modification, perfection
or certainty.

***The only requirement
for membership is the
desire to be loved.***

317 ■ YEAR

THERE IS NOTHING BETTER THAN BELONGING TO LOVE.

Instead of
PROVING PEOPLE WRONG,
how about proving
your worth and value
aren't tied to
PROVING PEOPLE WRONG.

Failure

doesn't circumvent success.

It allows your spirit
the opportunity
to bask in the

perfection of grace.

Grace allows you to stop being God.

GRACE DOES NOT MEASURE

FAILURE OR SUCCESS;

ONLY WHAT IS POSSIBLE IN LOVE.

322

YEAR

STOP RESISTING

THE MOMENT.

323
YEAR

YOU CAN BE RIGHT, BUT NOT EVERYONE NEEDS TO BE WRONG.

324
YEAR

CONTROL IS ISOLATION.

325 ■ YEAR

STUCK IS NOT A PLACE; IT'S A CHOICE

THE HUSTLE, THE GRIND,

are not your value or worth.

327 YEAR

HAVE AN OPINION ABOUT YOUR SOUL.

328 YEAR

PATROLLING THE BORDERS OF FAITH IS RACISM AND PREJUDICE.

329 YEAR

Spiritual transformation
is more a profession of ignorance
than of knowledge.

THE PARADOX
OF HEARING GOD:

KNOWING HE
HEARS YOU.

331
YEAR

Kill what keeps death alive.

Doubting and disowning *is all part of a magnificent faith.*

333 ■ YEAR

TEARS START THE JOURNEY.

334 ■ YEAR

IF YOU ARE IN THE SIN MANAGEMENT BUSINESS,

GET A NEW BUSINESS.

335
■ YEAR

CONTROL LOOKS LIKE JUDGMENT

ADVICE LOOKS LIKE WISDOM.

YOU ARE SEEKING WISDOM FROM PEOPLE,

NOT THEIR CONTROL.

337
YEAR

Spiritual responsibility:
Enlightening self,
community + earth
without prejudice.

338
YEAR

You are not the product
of humanity unhinged.
You are a creation of love.

AMBITION
BUILDS WALLS
BETWEEN
HEART AND **HAND.**

Your **"Why"** will never be satisfied.
Your **"How"** will always produce life.

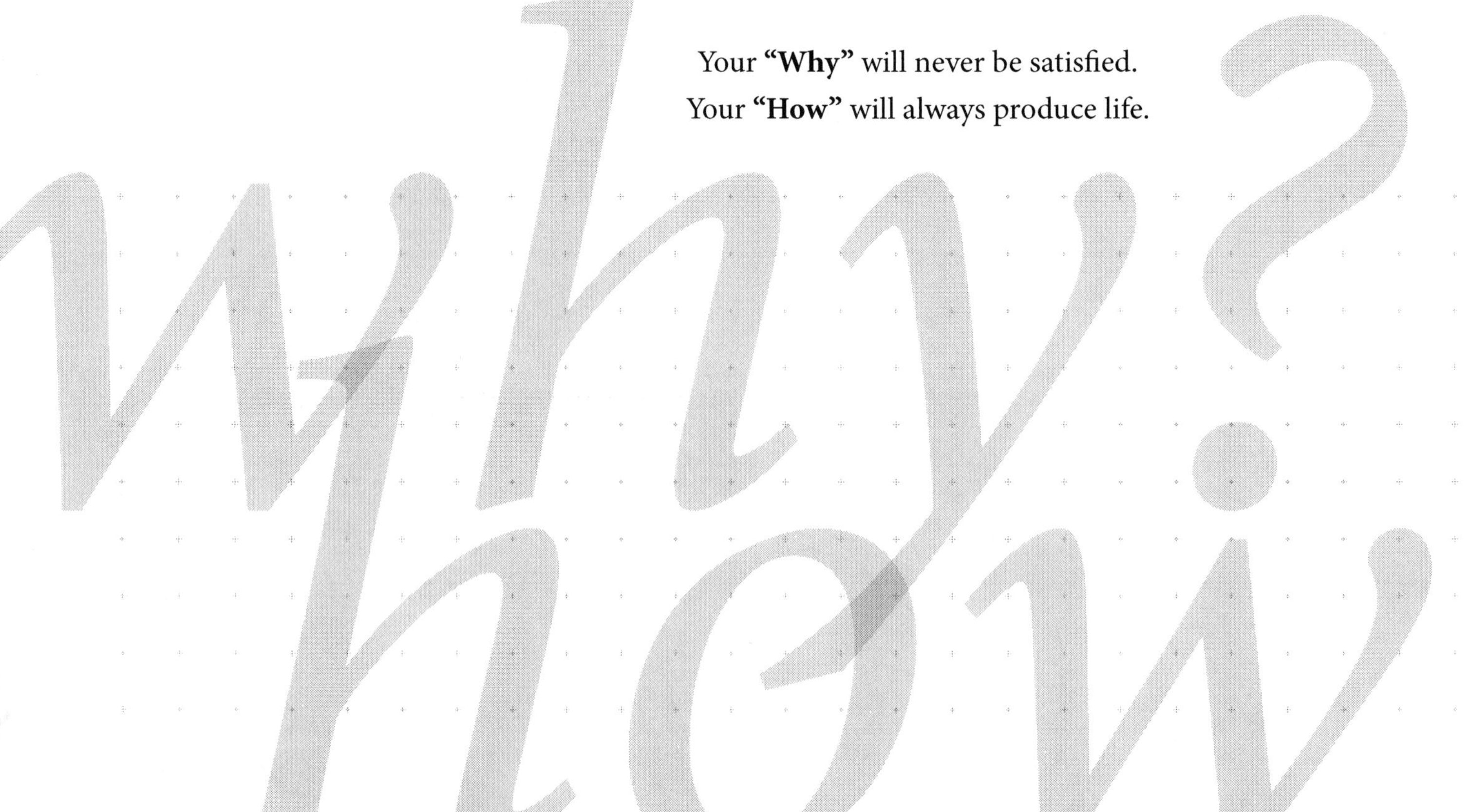

341 ■ YEAR

GOALS AREN'T DEADLINES.

NO FINISH

LINING LIFE.

343

YEAR

SEASONS
REQUIRE
DARKNESS.

Acceptance of love is the *condition of humility.*

345 YEAR

THE NAME-DROP

was invented by a terrified individual.

346 ■ YEAR

ACHIEVEMENT SHOULD NEVER SACRIFICE COMMUNITY.

347 YEAR

FAME IS NOT WISDOM.

Relationships
are not shelter.

349 ■ YEAR

Kill habitual responses.

BEING PISSED AT GOD IS A THING.

351 YEAR

Prayer is not formality. It's all day.

352 ■ YEAR

Preoccupation with getting is empty.

What do you think of yourself?

CREATE **SPIRITUAL PRACTICE**

Spiritual sarcasm is generated

from loneliness.

356 ■ YEAR

Every narrative is Jesus story.

357 YEAR

Jealousy ends when you celebrate its failure.

358 YEAR

Know your wounds.

---

359 YEAR

YOUR TABLE NEEDS STRANGERS.

360 ■ YEAR

Living apart from your ego produces freedom from self and the minds of others.

It will feel like shit for a season.

361

YEAR

The strength of your relationships hinge on

your willingness to forgive.

THE DOOR TO INTIMACY OPENS AS YOU STEP THROUGH THE FEAR OF BEING KNOWN.

Great intimacy

Great intimacy is

isn't great sex.

great vulnerability.

Reliance on people to move you ***EMOTIONALLY*** creates loneliness & desperation.

365
■ YEAR

Faith has seasons.

YOU WILL DOUBT.
YOU WILL EXPERIENCE.
YOU WILL DIE.
YOU WILL AWAKEN.
YOU WILL SACRIFICE.
YOU WILL HOLD TIGHT.
YOU WILL WALK.
YOU WILL RUN.
YOU WILL NEVER BE BORED.

J.R. MAHON

SPIRITUAL DIRECTOR / MENTOR

MY AIM FOR YOU

I'd like you to have nothing to prove and nothing to lose; liberated from ego, fear, and worry; at peace with who you are. I would love to be your spiritual director. Call or write for a session.

SPIRITUAL DIRECTOR

I've been a lot of things, but I've always been a spiritual director. The title can be super esoteric, leading some to think I have no spiritual boundaries or that I sit cross legged, humming, dressed in tie dye, smoking dope in the woods. Whatever your school of thought, I've found my voice among the mystics, meditators, contemplative silence-seeking dreamers who long for the love and touch of Trinity to permeate every corner of their being. Spiritual Direction takes the B.S. out of a relationship with God. It centers in the space between two people seeking the voice and movement of God. One person listening intently as another narrates the current season of life. Both people knowing God sits at the heart and center of the words and emotions. Spiritual direction seeks the intimacy of community, giving power to carry each other's burdens. A good spiritual director will have a spiritual director. A good spiritual director will help you hear your voice and identify true self. A good spiritual director will not make things easy. And lastly, a good spiritual director never steps into the spotlight that holds the Divine.

ABOUT J.R.

J.R. Mahon is a spiritual director, author, retreat leader and founder of TableTop Ministries. Mahon welcomes clients from all over the world in his spiritual direction practice, helping them connect and go deeper in relationship with the Divine. As spiritual director he counsels everything from spiritual formation, sexual abuse, addictions, the struggle with sexual orientation, grief and depression, and the battle of living with faith while chasing everything but. His passion is infectious and life changing.

J.R. leads quarterly workshops and conferences teaching people the discipline of spiritual direction.

The author of *Starving Jesus – Off the Pew, Into the World*, Mahon helped lead the early movement of XXXchurch as Executive Director and pastor.

Mahon is no stranger to engaging mass audiences, having spent 25 years in the television news business working as Executive Producer for Gannett Television, McGraw-Hill, E. W. Scripps Company and Tribune Broadcasting. Mahon is a highly skilled speaker, communicator, award-winning journalist and sought after creative consultant.

J.R. is married 25 years to his best friend Diane. They spend their time raising three adopted children and make their home in Southern California.

For speaking inquiries, private or group sessions with J.R.

jrmahon.com
jr@jrmahon.com
@jrmahon on social

619.964.0337

SUPAN CREATIVE CO.

Supan Creative was excited to partner with J.R. and TableTop Ministries to bring this project into existence. We love working with people whose goal is to impact people's lives and deepen their connection to Christ. If we can help you bring your vision into existance, we'd love to have that conversation. Contact us at sales@supans.com to discuss how we can put our team to work for you.

Made in the USA
Columbia, SC
13 November 2018